Do You Believe in Ninjas?

A Celebration of Ninjutsu in Verse

D.J. Kirkbride

illustrated by Chris Moreno

Do You Believe in Ninjas?
A Celebration of Ninjutsu in Verse
by D.J. Kirkbride
illustrated by Chris Moreno

Published in Canada by Creative Guy Publishing.
www.creativeguy.net
CGP-5011
ISBN-10: 1894953-762
ISBN-13: 978-1894953-764
November 2010
Trade edition

Library and Archives Canada Cataloguing in Publication

Kirkbride, D.J., 1977-
Do you believe in ninjas? : a celebration of ninjutsu in verse / D.J. Kirkbride.

Issued also in an electronic format.
ISBN 978-1-894953-76-4

I. Title.

PS3611.I753D69 2010   811'.6   C2010-906127-6

Do You Believe in Ninjas?

A Celebration of Ninjutsu in Verse

————————————————

D.J. Kirkbride

illustrated by Chris Moreno

creative guy publishing
vancouver | canada

This little book is
for all the ninjas of earth
dedication fear

Do You Believe In Ninjas?

Do you believe in ninjas, little girl?

Do you believe in ninjas in your worl'?

I do. You should, too.
Ninjas are all around us.
They specialize in being... invisible.

So if the ninja is a good ninja,
You wouldn't know if he (or she) was around.

Don't be dumb.

Ninjas are all around us.

Ninjas Are People, Too

Ninjas are people, too.
       Those silent warriors in their jammies
       of a dark hue.

Sure, they wear silly footwear.
       The way the big toe's
       separated from the other toes.

But can you jump fitty feet in the air?

I doubt it, bee-yatch.

忍者 4

Do Ninjas Love?

Do ninjas love?
   Do they have time... for love... ?

Ninjas are all about invisibility, but...
   are their hearts... invisible?

Can ninjas turn off their emotions
   as easily as they can... disappear?

Oh, woe begone, God bless the lonely,
   lonely... ninjas.

Zeus Respects Ninjas

One time Zeus
      (yeah, King of the Greek gods)
      was in Asgard,
            chilling with Odin
            (yeah, King of the Norse gods)
They used to hang out
      every month,
      and last month was in
            Valhalla, so
      it was Odin's turn to host.
Anyway, as per usual,
      they kicked back with their
            mead and a quick toast.
And then just started
            talking smack on humans,
      looking down on them
      from yonder heavens.
But when Odin made
      fun of a ninja,
            something about
      wearing silly pajamas—
            Zeus said, "NAY!!!"
He threw down his
mead and told Odin that
      ain't no one disses ninjas.

Odin was shocked,
     and the one-eyed brawler
         put up his godly dukes!
Surely such a fight
     would cause the Heavens to rumble
     and the Earth to crumble.
But then they realized…
     … somethin' wasn't right.
When Odin asked what they were
     about to fight about…
Zeus said, "Thou dissed ninjas!"
Thing is, Odin digs on ninjas, too.
But he'd said…
But what?
But wait…
"LOKI, thou makest
     the most annoying trouble!"
        Odin shouted at his adopted son.
'Fore even the gods,
don't find it fun…
…
To diss on…
THE NINJA.

7　　　　　　　　　　　　　　　　　　　　忍者

A Ninja's Inner Demons

Sometimes a ninja
      has some inner demons

Can't use kicks and chops
      to fight his own feelin's.

When, after a long day of ninjatics
and assassinating acrobatics,
he's got no email,
      especially not from a female...

That kinda sucks,
      but 'least he has his nunchucks,
and he can disappear in a cloud o' smoke—
      c'mon, these skills ain't no joke.

But, yeah, a ninja can get sad.
      But, still, bein' a ninja is pretty rad.

忍者

Ninjas Play The Lotto

Ninjas play the lotto,
    though it's not about luck.

Ninjas play the lotto
    'cause they don't give a fuck.

When you get paid to kill
and are good at your job,
a few dollars on some
silly lotto tickets
    really ain't worth two shits.

And if that ninja wins,
easy money still spends,
and he can always use
another sword or nun-
    chuck.

忍者

Ninjas Are In Your Heart

Ninjas are in your heart.
Yeah, every organ has to do its part.
If a ninja was in your thigh...
that isn't an organ, so it don't
apply.

Ninjas don't care about your dreams,
and they don't live in your
spleens.

Ninjas are stronger than your soul,
and, like you, they eat cereal
and milk
out of a bowl.

Ninjas are in your heart,
which is more important than
any
other
part...

... of YOU!

Dude, a ninja could eat your HEART!

忍者

Ninjas Don't Matter

Ninjas don't matter none
    'cause ninjas ain't no
        fun.

Ninjas ain't drinkin' rum
    'cause ninjas ain't no
        fun.

Ninjas don't need no gun
    'cause ninjas—

are fierce warriors who use swords and
throwing stars and their own bodies as
    weapons (!)
thusly needing no modern contrivances
or doo-dads that make killing easy
    and impersonal.

Ninjas DO matter, son.

Haiku Slam, no. 1

A ninja can fly
Like a free bird in the sky
Even without wings

Sits on golden pond
Ninja on a lily pad
Frog-like assassin

Nunchuck to the face
Don't diss a ninja's cooking
Eggs runny or no

Sand clouding eyesight
Black suit hot in desert sun
Poor thirsty ninja

Haunted By Ninjas

Ninjas.
They haunt my every moment,
always seeming to be just outside my peripheral
vision.
Infiltrating my dreams,
both sleeping and...
waking.

I never feel alone,
a strange pins and needles feeling on the back of my
neck,
like there's someone behind me at all times...
someone wearing black pajamas complete with a
mask and footies that separate the big toe from the
little toes for reasons I'll never understand.

When I turn, I see nothing...
but I know I didn't just imagine it.
Why, though?
Why are they shadowing me?
I don't recall wronging anyone,

忍者   **14**

but there's no other reason I'd be tailed by ninjas
other than someone hired them to chop me loose
the mortal coil.
They must be biding their time.
Any day now,
a swift kick to the head or throwing star to the
jugular could have my name on it.

I wish I knew what I'd done to deserve this,
but it's not a terrible way to go.
It's actually kind of cool.
I'd prefer old age, though.

Ninjas Are Caffeine Junkies

Ninjas are caffeine junkies
to ninjas coffee is like
bananas is to monkeys.

A ninja is best cloaked by the shadow of night,
he gotta stay awake into the wee hours
to best his opponents through surprise in a fight.

To do this, some ninjas sleep during the day,
and do their assassinating during night,
but some take day jobs, so that's not the best way.

These poor bastards have to stay up almost 24/7,
so they drink coffee to keep their fool asses awake,
so that
daytime and night they can send their victims to
hell or heaven.

While many folks take their coffee with sugar and
cream,
ninjas just need that jolt and don't get all frivolous,
taking their coffee black as the darkest ninja dream

Bottom line is that ninjas
like their coffee really strong;
they don't mess around, suckas.

忍者

Ninjas Love Gold

Ninjas love them some gold.
> It ain't just for pirates,
> or so I done been told.

If ninjas are one thing,
> it's lethal.
If they are two things,
> they're lethal and greedy.
If they are three things,
> they're lethal, greedy, and stylish...

Dressed smartly in black
> for their silent attack.

But their attire costs money...
> You think Tabi boots are cheap?
> Maybe in your magic dreams whilst you
sleep.

Being butt ass broke gets old,
> so that's why ninjas,
> much like their pirate arch-nemeses,
>> or Leprechauns (the ninja's
>> secret immortal frienemies)
> love them some gold!

忍者   **18**

Ninjas Tolerate Lactose

Ninjas tolerate lactose.
    Physical superiority
        is a priority;
    Ninjas know milk does the body good,
        and drink it like they should.

Ninjas DO NOT tolerate
    being captured by an enemy,
        thinkin' hari kari.
    When escape doesn't seem possible,
        take a cyanide pill.

But ninjas love to eat cheese.
    To not tolerate lactose would make
        it very hard to take.
    So a ninja knows dairy is great,
        easy to tolerate.

But fuck being held captive by an enemy.
Seriously.

忍者

Officer Ninja

If a ninja becomes a
        cop,
you know crime in his town would
        stop.

A ninja upholding the
        law.
The other cops would watch in
        awe.

And the bullet budget would
        drop,
throwing stars for a ninja
        cop.

Winning fights,
reading rights,
        protecting the nights.

Haiku Slam, no. 2

Black ninja footies
Big toe shan't touch little toes
Footprint of your doom

Many ways to kill
With or without a weapon
Ninja equals death

Ninjas watch football
they love the competition
and the tight, tight pants

Ninjas love to Tweet
When they kick you with their feet
Ninjas got you beat

忍者

Real Ninjas Rock Corndogs

Real ninjas rock corndogs,
    not a second thought given
    to the lips and hooves of hogs.
        The bigger and fatter,
        dipped in tasty cornbatters—
        curing hunger's what matters.

Clever ninjas dig corndogs
    'cause they a meal on a
        stick...
    which makes a handy weapon
        right quick...
    when lunch is over and some
        surly dick...
    tries to catch them unawares,
        failing to recognize that
          deadly corndog stick.

The best ninjas know corndogs
    are some tasty lunchtime snacks
    complete with a wooden spear,
    handy for stabbing in a
    would-be assassin's thorax.

Real ninjas ROCK corndogs.

Fear The Ninja

Is you afraid of ninjas,
        little punk?
Bes' say yes 'fore one kicks you
        in the junk.

Yeah, ninjas are plenty cool,
        but they don't follow no rule.
To a ninja, you're just a
        silly, little, no good tool.
And for you not to fear 'em
        makes your punk ass nuthin' but
        one soon to be dead-ass fool.

Now, before a throwing star
        flies at your head from afar,
Let me ask you one more time:
        Is you afraid of ninjas...
            ...after this scary-ass rhyme?

忍者

Will You Be This Ninja's Friend?

Will you be this ninja's friend?
    Hang with him
    until the
    bitter end?

Can you be this ninja's soul mate?
    Talkin' 'bout
    life, stayin'
    up real late?

Would you give this ninja a dolla'?
    and fitty
    cent? So he
    has bus fare?

What?? This isn't just about money, dog!
    Sometimes some
    ninjas ain't
    get no pay!

C'mon!!! Have a heart and be this ninja's frien'!!!

Drinks With A Ninja

You took a ninja drinking?
What the hell were you THINKING?

No wonder you have
      a nunchuck
      concussion.

Lucky he didn't
kill no one.

…

Oh, he did?
Well, you got
      a ninja
      straight up drunk.
So stupid.

Ninjas and booze?
Of course you lose.

忍者

Ninjas Don't Give A Hoot

Ninjas don't give a hoot.
Mess with one of 'em or
even look at them wrong,
they'll kick you right in the
poop shoot.

Because ninjas don't give
a fuck about shit, dude.
They'll puncture your thorax
or knock out your teeth if
you're rude.

Ninjas defy social
niceties in that they
will not take crap from you,
be you Black, White, Asian,
or Jew.

If you ain't got no class,
ninjas will beat your ass...
For true.

What Up With Ninjas?

What up with ninjas?
    For true.

What crawled up their butts
    and died?

They momma told 'em
    they cute...

        But she lied.

Is that why they wear
    masks?

To cover up they
    ugly,
    fugly
    faces?

Is that why they dig
    killing with
    Ninjutsu?

Since they're so ugly,
    they gotta
    be angry,
    too?

What up with ninjas?

忍者

I Saw A Fat Ninja

I saw a fat ninja
walkin' down the street,
cankles above his
fat fuckin' feet.

This ninja was portly,
thunder thighs makin'
friction, smell the smoke,
fat legs rubbin'.

I saw a fat ninja—
how can he jump high?
My torso isn't
as big as his

right fuckin' thunder thigh.

Fat ninja should exercise.

忍者

忍者

Haiku Slam, no. 3

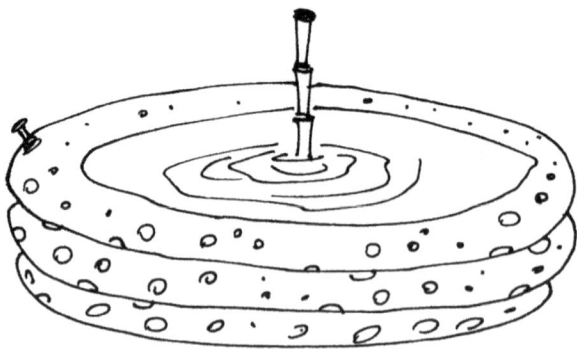

Ninjas don't drink beer
It's loss of control they fear
And they can do flips

Ninjas like bacon
You know ninjas ain't fakin'
Takin' your bacon

Some ninjas have cars
Ninjutsu behind the wheel
Get your oil changed

My ninja haiku
might not be legit haiku
but ninjas are cool

Ninjas All Up In It

Ninjas get all up in it.
You even cross 'em
You're gonna be in some
Shit.

Ninjas take a target down.
To get in the way
You'd have to be a foo'
Clown.

Ninjas gonna fuck you up.
Mess wit' 'em, dumbass,
And you be shit outta
Luck.

Ninjas?
Fuck, dude,
They All Up In It!

忍者

Could You Love A Ninja?

Could you ... love a ninja?

Could you hold a
    ninja in your arms
    and console him after
    an assassination attempt
    on the czar of some foreign land
    has gone awry?
        ... And just let him cry?

Could you nod and smile
    when your ninja silently, invisibly
    comes down the stairs
    in the morning for breakfast
    and eats the scrambled eggs
    and pancakes you prepared—
        without so much as a "Thank you"
        ... just grabbing his sais and leaving
        dirty dishes behind?

SHOULD you ... love a ninja?

忍者

Ninja In Crisis

Ninjas have moments of
      emotional crisis

Questioning their
      self-worth

Dealing with ninjatic stress,
      under kicking duress

But they fight through it.

Ninjas Get The Sniffles

Ninjas get the sniffles—
it's rare, but it's
true.

Ninjas are just human—
though stronger and
much faster than
you.

But when it's cold outside,
and the ninja's
immune system
is kinda run
down...

Ninjas get the sniffles—
like you and me,
too.

The Day a Ninja Cried

The day a ninja cried,
    Was the day part o' my soul
        DIED.

The day a ninja cried,
    I knew that my daddy had
        LIED.

The way that ninja cried,
    Just made me feel sick in...
        SIDE.

When a ninja's bottom lip
    Started to quiver,
    You couldn't see it
    Due to his ninja mask...
    But you could FEEL it,
        and it felt like SHIT.

When that ninja's eyes
    Filled with tough guy lies
    And got all teary and bleary
    And welled up, it was sad
    And embarrassing and creepy
        For seri.

One day a ninja balled
    His eyes out after
    Stubbing his toesy woesy...
    Like a baby waybe...
    It's a day that will forever be called
        Totally lame.

That day a ninja cried...
    The day I wish I'd never
    TRIED.

        To live
        To believe
        To be.

The day a ninja cried,
    My weary soul gave up and
        DIED.

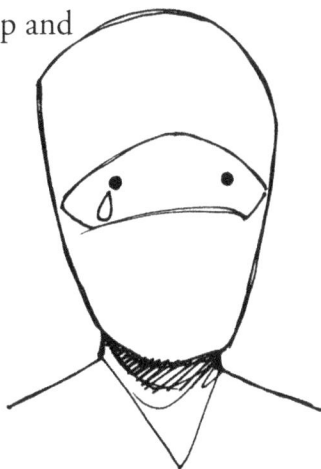

忍者

Ninjas Go To The Dentist

Ninjas get nervous
        at the dentist
                just like the rest of us.

Every six months they
        get their check up,
        and then nature's roles…
                … reverse.

Pain dealers
        are dealt pain.
                In the *mouth*.

        It is…
                … perverse.

Does not matter how much
        they brush
        and floss
        and rinse,

the scraping and picking
        and scraping (yeah, twice mentioned)
        make even ninjas wince.

But do ninjas *fear* the dentist?
        Uh, no, I wouldn't go that far.

Old Man Ninja

The little old man
bought some Dapper Dan
at the grocery store.

In the parking lot,
some punks took a shot—
tried to rob the old man.

They learned a lesson
all about messin'
'cause none was guessin'
that this senior citizen...
    knew mad ninjutsu.

Look past the wrinkles,
beyond liver spots,
around the gray hair...
    Though it is quite rare,
Ninjas *can* get old.

He'll just need a nap
after he's kicked the crap
outta you punk kids.

Respect your elders...
    'specially NINJAS.

忍者

45   忍者

Haiku Slam, no. 4

When ninjas need sleep
they crane kick insomnia
it beats counting sheep

Ninjas have birthdays
yes, they are human like you
except way tougher

Ninja kicks your ass
do not get down on yourself
they are super tough

Ninjas pop and lock
but don't expect a moonwalk
that's the King of Pop

Ninjas Don't Dig Improv

When ninjas wants to see
        some comedy,
improv is not their first choice.

While when done right
        it can be a delight,
        it usually sucks,
        and makes a ninja want
                to use nunchucks.

Everyone likes to laugh,
        but improve is hit and miss—
        and, unlike a ninja,
                usually miss.

Ninjas don't dig this.

Deadly blow dart to the neck!
What— ?
Don't break character!
Wait, he's not faking…
Did that blow dart come from the audience???

Improv your way out of *that*!

忍者   **48**

When Ninjas Drink Too Much Coffee

When ninjas drink too much coffee,
     their teeth take on the color of toffee.

A belly full of this fine-ass roast,
     ain't always something of which to boast.

Dig it: ninjas have to be stealthy...
     ...quiet and sneaky to stay healthy...
     ...and if they kill for money, to get wealthy.

But drinking coffee effs with their digestion...
     Weird noises abound,
     causing sneaking around,
     without making a sound,
     kinda out of the question.

That type of noisy stomach shit could get a ninja
killed, man.

SHHHHHHHHHH!

Ninjas should not drink too much coffee.

The Last Time A Ninja Ran For President

The last time a ninja ran for president
he won.

His name was George.
George Washington.

Turns out high end
assassination
pays way better than
leading a nation,

so this was the first and last
time that it happened.

But it DID happen.

忍者

Don't Give Coal to a Ninja

Don't put no coal in
a ninja's stockin'
on Christmas mornin'.
    No matter how bad he been.

Santa rides a sleigh
eve of Christmas day
slides down chimney way,
    ever silent, so they say.

But a ninja can
detect that fat man.
Ninja know when San-
    ta's reindeer is gonna lan'.

So if good St. Nick
don't want ninja kick
in his flaccid dick
    his presents best do the trick.

Ninja good or no,
Claus, if you put coa'
in his stocking, yo...
    You'll meet your death, ho, ho, ho.

Ninjas In Da Basement

What's that sound?
...
Exactly.
It's quiet.

    Too quiet.

Nothing, not even
    a stirring
In the entire
    gee-damn house.

    Fuck, dude.

Ninjas? Why would they want us?
What'd be their
       motivation?

Wait!!! Did you hear that?

Like a slice through the
      air?
... Hey, I'm talkin' to
      you!

Now did you or did you not
         hear that?

Dude?
...
Dude?

Oh sh—!

Ninja Hunger

It's hard to order
        a burrito
When you're practically
        invisible.

This is the plight of
        hungry ninja.

Yeah, it's the same for
        every food,
Be it a burger
        or some pizza.

Due to stealth training
        and living in the
        shadow killzone,
It's easy to
        miss a hungry
        ninja ordering
Some tasty eats.

Ninja Joe (Hearts) Ninja Flo

Ninja Joe
meets Miss Ninja Flo
at a Ninjutsu Bar in Weho,
and whaddya know?

Ninja Joe digs Ninja Flo—
asks her out for a burrito.
He's nervous she'll say "No,"
but she's all, "Fo' sho'."

Soon they see each other mo' 'n mo'!
    They go to a show,
    They eat cookie dough,
    They assassinate a pirate named Pirate Poe,
    They even make ninja angels in the snow!

Before he knows it, Ninja Joe loves Ninja Flo!
He even moves into her tidy condo...
but Ninja Joe is a man ho,
and he cheats on Ninja Flo
with a Ninja flooz named Ninja Bo,

So Miss Ninja Flo cries, "You gots ta' GO,
    Ninja Joe!"

It's A Male Ninja's World

It's a male ninja's worl'
    Be tougher for a ninja
        GIRL.

A ninja fella can chill
    When he's done with his assigned
        KILL.

But the poor ninja lady
    Has to balance her career
    With her growing family
    And her unappreciative
        Hubby
    Making supper and cleaning,
    Nurturing her lil' children,
    Taking care of her boorish
        Husban'
    On top of her ninjatic
        Duty,
    Silently killing peeps for
        Honor.
    (Actually it's for... MONEY.)

忍者

She gotsta work twice as hard
    As some lazy guy ninja
        Retard.

No, it ain't fair or modern
    But most ninjas are just old-
        Fashioned.

It's a male ninja's WORLD.

Haiku Slam, no. 5

sneak. sneak. sneak.

Ninjas love to dance
and you know they're good at it
because they're ninjas?

Ninjas are not fools
even if it's April 1st
you cannot trick them

Ninjas are not born
they are made via training
life of ass kicking

I love my brown Chucks
nothing to do with ninjas
they've fallen apart

忍者

Sometimes Ninjas Do Stupid Things

Sometimes ninjas do stupid things.
They don't always know what's wrong and what's
what and what's right...
    Especially when they're not in a fight.

Sometimes, it takes someone to go, "You're being
totally stupid right now,"
    For them to see the light.

Sometimes the things a ninja does could be thought
of as stupid.
A ninja might be susceptible to peer pressure
    And find himself acting a fool for good measure.
    And his ninja friend goes, "Say, buddy, what the
hell are you doin'?"
    And he stops, thinks, and replies, "Whoa. Yeah.
I'm not sure."

Sometimes a ninja doesn't think before action,
doing things that are considered stupid.

Like drink toilet water on a dare
Or wear his ninja friend's used underwear
Or remove the stubble on his face with Nair
Or wash that distinguished gray right out of his
hair.

Sometimes ninjas do stupid things.
    Because they're only human, too...
    Just like me or you...

Only they can kick through brick walls
And swiftly remove an enemy's balls
And be totally invisible, even in empty halls.

Yes, ninjas are better than us.

But it's obvious
    that they're not perfect...
            For serious.

Ninjas In Space

Ninjas in space,
Whose side are they on?

Are they defending us from alien invaders?
Or are they Ninjutsu Darth Vaders?

I mean, what if they were up there,
In their astro-ninja-underwear,
Planning our downfall?
The global death of us all?

That's probably the deal.
Ninjas freaking hate humanity.
At least that's how I was raised to…
… raised… to… feel… ?

Holy shit.
Wait a minute.

Was I raised to hate ninjas?
To be a ninja hater?

忍者 **62**

No, I don't blame Mom and Dad.
It's society that's bad.
The media, that's who to blame...
... for my ninja-hating shame.

Just because they can kill me with a kick,
Doesn't mean I have to be a dick.

Ninjas, on earth or in space,
Are part of the human race.

So, I'm going to hug a ninja, and—ack!
I was just stabbed... with a ninja... sword...
... what a sneaky ninja attack.

Lesson learned?

Probably not.

忍者

Ninjas Don't Jazzercise

Ninjas don't jazzercise
        to keep the thunder out of their thighs.
                For that they kick tons of ass.

Ninjas don't diet
        as a way to stay fit.
                Badass assassinations keep 'em thin.

Ninjas don't sweat to the oldies
        to be free of ass-fat foldies.
                Airborne flipping is better than
Richard Simmons' moves.

Ninjas don't jazzercise,
        or freaking diet,
                or sweat to no oldies.

Ninjas
kick
ass.

        Which is wonderful exercise.

Ninjas Don't Fade Away

Ninjas never fade quietly away
   into the calm night.
For the strong, proud, badass ninja that just
   doesn't seem alright.

While ninjas are quite silent assassins
   and pass unnoticed,
they ain't wanna get all feeble and old.
   That's shit, truth be told.

Ninjas live really big, exciting lives,
   though in the shadows.
But they are people with people's needs and
   live it up like ho's.

Ain't no way a ninja would fade away
   when it's his last day.

Like Jon Bon Jovi
   ninjas go down in a blaze of glory.

Ninjas Hate Traffic

Though professional
     when they are hired
     to kick you to death,
     ninjas sometimes get
          emotional.
A ninja rage
     is never more real
     than when stuck in traffic,
          behind the wheel.
Ninjas don't hesitate,
     but many drivers do;
     waiting too long at a green light
     breeds ninja hate,
          whether wrong or right.
Ninjas can kick people,
     but they wish they could
     kick bad traffic.
          Kick its ass.

忍者   **66**

Ninjas Aren't Tree Huggers

A tree
might be
lovely.

But a
ninja
can knock it down with one freaking kick.

Sucka.

Mustachioed Ninja

Ninja with a mustache,
>   your hairy lip aids you in the kicking
>   of ass.

Whatever your reason for growing your 'stache,
>   it works for you.
>   I say this true blue.

Show off your 'stache,
>   and cut a 'stache hole in your mask...
>   In fear your enemies will bask.

Show off that sweet hairy lip...
>   Oh! And when you kick,
>   remember to pivot with your hip.

Look, put that razor down.
>   Without that god-given 'stache,
>   you look like a child clown.

Ninja, sweet mustachioed ninja,
      you beautiful bastard,
      don't ever give up the dream.

Shaving your lip
      won't make your enemies scream
          ... in terror.

忍者

Haiku Slam, no. 6

Now I must slumber
though the ninjas may attack
before I wake up

Don't give a ninja
some dang computer virus
ninja will kick you

Cannot fake ninja
ninja is a state of mind
with lots of kicking

Cell phone reception
is important to ninja.
Dropped calls equal death.

忍者

Why Ninjas?

Why ninjas?

Why not ninjas?
     I'll tell ya' why not—
     They're wearing nothing
     More than glorified pajamas.

And we're 'sposed ta' fear 'em?

Here's what I think o'
Them damn sissy ninjas—
URK! Oh my— my throat—

Japanese throwing star—
To— my— throat—

Damn— ninjas...

忍者 **72**

Ninja Always Beats Robot

A ninja be tougher
    than a silly ass robot.
Badass ninjutsu skillz
    beat what a metal "man" got.

'Lectric gizmos, gadgets,
    and whatnot don't mean nuthin'
to a well trained ninja
    with nunchucks and high kickin'.

Sure a 'bot is metal,
    created by mad science...
But a ninja's got soul
    and can attack in silence.

Fancy robot sensors
    can't detect ninja attacks
until it's far too late—
    sharp throwing star in its back.

Ninja always beats robot.

Ninja At The Door

Knock-knock
Who's th—
       GAK!

Sai in
my chest…
       ack…

Ninja
at the
door

always
equals
       DEATH.

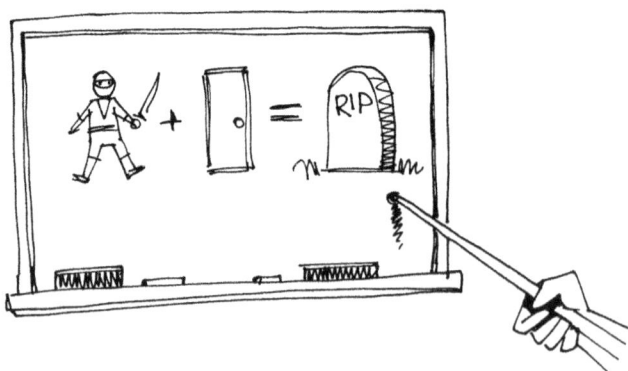

Ninjas Don't Do Medium

Silently killing for a living
          is extreme.
It is the ninja's way.

Ordering a medium soda
          is wishy-washy,
which ain't okay.

If a ninja orders steak,
          it's rare or it's well done.
                    Medium?
                    Medium well?
                    Medium rare?
          A ninja ain't having none
                    (of that).

A ninja goes fast.
A ninja creeps slow.
          A medium pace?
                    No, no.

Ninjas do NOT do medium,
                    son.

*(I realize this is a weird way
to tell you I am your father.)*

Ninja Footwear

Ninja footwear
Should fit a
Ninja's foot
Not like a
Glove.

Ninja footwear
Should fit a
Ninja's foot
Like a
      MITTEN.

Don't want that big
Toe to even TOUCH
Them other toes,
Love.

      'Cause, y'a see…
It's not comfortable
To a ninja foot,
      Kitten.

Ninjas Don't Drink Alone

When a ninja has a
      thirst
It's usually for sweet
      death.
But sometimes he wants a
      buzz.

Though to drink in soli-
      tude…
Even when he's in the
      mood
Isn't really all that
      safe.

Ninja must be in con-
      trol,
Lest he cause a high death
      toll…
For which he gets no mon-
      ey.

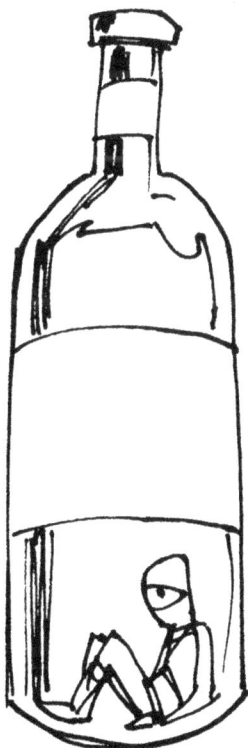

忍者

A Ninja Prepares A Sandwich

When a ninja hits the kitchen
       (to cook, not for a chef-related
                 assassination)

He takes his food prep
       seriously.

Tomatoes are sliced with precision
       (to be fair, everything is sliced with
                 precision)
       (lettuce, meat, cheese)

Onions are diced with efficiency
       (and not a tear is shed,
       for a ninja's tear ducts
       are said to be dead—
       a gift or a curse,
               depending upon your
               interpretation)

Basically, ninjas make kickass sandwiches.

忍者

When A Ninja Buys Booze Without Getting Carded

Sometimes a ninja
just has to unwind.

Going to a bar
by rooftop or car
      can be an option.

Some beers with his friends
with no violence
      can be relaxing.

But when that ninja
gets a mimosa
      and is not carded…

The ninja feels old;
his heart grows so cold…
which makes him drink more.

Moviegoing Ninjas

Ninjas
going to the cinemas
don't pay like us suckas.

They stick to the shadows,
hiding where no one knows.

Up on the ceiling like flies,
in the places beyond our eyes.

Ninja sneak
to get a movie peek.

But maybe you'll see one getting a snack,
if they have a munchy attack.

Ninja buying soda
at the cinema,
and putting butter on their popcorn.

忍者

忍者

Someone's Watchin' You, Santa

Ninjas were once kids...
Little gals and boys
who made their wish lists
for fun Christmas toys.

Young ninja Sacha,
he was one such kid...
but Santa disliked
something Sacha did.*

Because his wish for
a nice set of sais
and ninja smoke bombs
garnered no replies.

忍者   **82**

Sacha was denied
for reasons unknown,**
but look out, Santa,
'cause Sacha has grown...

Into a master NINJA.

Santa decides the
naughty and the nice,
but a ninja kills
without thinking twice.

*Sacha stole a classmate's lunch money.
** Not true, see the above note.

忍者

Ninjas Don't Get Healthcare

Ninjas don't get healthcare.
  See that line over there?
  That's the free health clinic
    where them people without
    insurance have to go
    when they get hurt or sick.

Ninjas don't get health care.
  They say that it's not fair,
  but theirs is a risky
    profession, and those dark,
    violent assassins
    companies won't carry.

Ninjas don't get healthcare.
  Can't see them standing there
  because they are hiding
    in plain sight, but there are
    ninjas with colds and sai
    wounds in that line waiting.

Waiting... for some healthcare.

Ninjas Don't Get Pissed

Ninjas don't get pissed
   Even when they throw a star
      At at human target...
AND THEY MUH-FUCKING MISS!

Ninjas don't get down
   Even when betrayal is
      The true name o' the game...
THEY FUCKING GET EVEN!

Ninjas don't get fool
   Though their footies sure ain't cool,
      They make a lot of sense...
AND THEY KICK ALL KINDS O'

...ass.

Ninjas Hate To Pay For Parking

If a ninja has to drive
            to an assassination
                    gig,

Paying for parking
            is something a ninja don't
                    dig.

Finding parking in the city
            is bad enough,
but to expect a ninja to pay for it?

        TOUGH.

A Ninja On The Edge

It's hard to unwind
when around every corner
      you might find
            Death.

Chilling out and relaxing
even during your free time
      tends to become taxing
      when you can kick through
            Brick.

So if a ninja seems on edge,
don't be belligerent and
      push him over the ledge,
            Friend.

Because if he can kick through brick,
your skull won't seem that
            Thick.

忍者

Don't Talk During A Ninja's Favorite Show

Don't talk during a ninja's favorite show!
What are you?
A dodo?

      He'll kill you fo' sho'!

Sitcom, drama, reality—
Don't distract the relaxing ninja
from the TV.

It's a rare thing to find,
but sometimes even a ninja
      has to unwind,
by shutting down
        his mind.

Ninjas Don't Lose (Fights)

When I was told
        a ninja lost
                a fight,

I knew in my baboon
        heart something was
                not right.

The only time a ninja
        would lose a fight
        is with another ninja,
                and in that scenario
                a ninja still won
                that fight,
                        sooooo…
Semantics.

忍者

Ninjas Don't Dance At Weddings

The title of this poem
　　　　is a lie.

Ninjas rarely marry, but
sometimes they do.
　　　　Wedded ninjutsu.

And if a ninja has to get dressy,
the reception's gonna get messy.

Dancin' can involve kickin'
　　　　and flippin'.
Ninja dance is straight trippin'.

And a lucky bridesmaid
　　　　might get ninja laid…
　　　　　　　So long as it's consensual.
　　　　　　　Ninja attraction, mutual.

Ninja Arm Wrestling

Ninja arm wrestling
is even more intense than it sounds.

Dramatic stalemates,
ninja arm wrestlers sitting their grounds.

Arm wrestling action,
as a ninja goes "over the top."

One arm is winning,
but the other is ready to chop.

Usually this sport
doesn't involve smoke bombs, flips, and kicks...

Ninja arm wrestling
is spruced up with crazy ninja tricks.

忍者

Ninjas Are Good Listeners

If you have a tale to tell,
    if you need to get something off your chest,
        if something is eating you up inside, but...
... you've no one to talk to...

Just start talking.
Right now.
In your room
    or car
        or wherever you are.

Because science has proven
    that there is likely a ninja near.

We're never alone
    when there are shadows and fear.

Ninjas won't reply,
    but they'll let you talk.

And even if they've been hired to kill you,
    well... you won't have anything to whine about.

Because you'll be dead.

Holiday Superiority

When the bodies were found,
the Bunny and Santa on the ground,
there was no evidence.

But this wasn't done by chance.

An anonymous client
who was a financial giant,
put a hit on these icons.

And he hired a ninja.

Clearly not messing around,
the ninja's work was sound,
and now the number one holiday
is Valentine's Day.

Don't be stupid,
the client was Cupid.

Turkeys and leprechauns...
watch your backs.

忍者   94

Ninjas: Why Do I Love Them So?

Ninjas...

Why do I love them so?
      If I was around them
      I'd become a ho.

Ninjas...

Why are they so damn cool?
      Compared to their greatness
      I feel like a tool.

Haiku Slam

—fin—

Best check your voicemail.
Is there a ninja message?
You are so dead, dude.

A ninja email
is lurking in your inbox—
email spam of death.

Ninja handwriting
is not as elegant as
assassinating.

High kick or low kick,
a ninja will beat you up.
Don't lie to yourself.

Acknowledgments

My ninja poetry lived for some time on the famed internet before being printed on paper. Many of the poems in this book debuted on these fine websites: thefootnote.net, tlchicken.com, and djkirkbride.com.

Thanks go to those sites for internetting these ninja poems… except for djkirkbride.com, because that's my own bloggy site, and it'd be weird to thank myself.

Many sincere thanks, however, must go to Adam P. Knave, who not only wrote the haiku gracing the back cover, but also put this whole adventure into motion, by introducing me to Pete S. Allen and Creative Guy Publishing. He's a swell fella, as is Pete. I offer my highest of high fives to both of them, as well as to Chris Moreno, for it is he who decorated this book with his excellent illustrations.

And finally, thanks to my family for never telling me that writing something like a book of ninja poetry was a dumb idea. They probably thought it, but they never said it. To me, anyway.

About the Author

D.J. Kirkbride has written stories for all four volumes of the POPGUN comic book anthology from Image Comics, often with his collaborator, Adam P. Knave. He was also on the editorial team for all four books, winning the 2008 Harvey Award and the 2010 Eisner Award for Best Anthology.

Additionally, D.J. is the editor of THE NEW BRIGHTON ARCHEOLOGICAL SOCIETY, KILL ALL PARENTS, AQUA LEUNG (Image Comics), and the webcomic SPY6TEEN (spy6teen.com).

All that is well and good, but one must note that he's been writing poems and haiku about ninjas for years.

Years.

Seriously… years. More of his writing can be found on his bloggy website, djkirkbride.com.

Believe in your dreams.

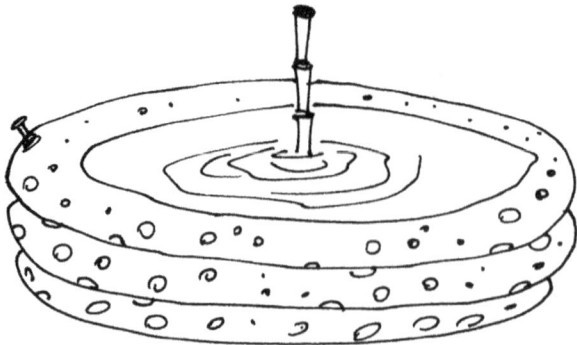

忍者

About the Artist

Chris Moreno is the creator of the comic "Sanz Pantz: Ninja Platypus" that appeared in the Eisner Award-winning POPGUN anthologies from Image Comics.

D.J. Kirkbride was an editor on the Eisner Award-winning POPGUN anthologies from Image Comics in which "Sanz Pantz: Ninja Platypus" appeared.

D.J. Kirkbride has written this book of ninja poetry that Chris Moreno has illustrated. Some would say that this was fated to be; others would say this is mere coincidence.

Still others would say, "Who are you? Leave me alone." It is left to the reader to divine some arcane meaning from these facts.

In addition to being guided by the hand of Fate, Chris Moreno has worked on comics from almost every publisher in comics, from Marvel to IDW, on books such as WORLD WAR HULK: FRONT LINE, Paul Jenkins' SIDEKICK, TOY STORY, and MOTEL HELL.

He's also the creator of the webcomic DYSFUNCTIANIMALS (dysfunctianimals.blogspot.com) and the upcoming ZOMBIE DICKHEADS. You can find more of his art on his website, chrismoreno.org.

Chris Moreno lives and works in North Hollywood, California, not too far from D.J. Kirkbride. Coincidence?

You decide.